Tumor Boy

Merrily ~
Thanks for being
my hospital angel

10/19/2012

[signature]

Tumor Boy

John J. Healy

To order additional copies of this book, contact:
Xlibris Corporation
1-888-795-4274
www.Xlibris.com
Orders@Xlibris.com
121215

FOREWARD

I am proud to be a brain tumor survivor—certainly not something everyone or even most peope can list as an accomplishment. I am also proud now to be a published author. I just hope that this book helps someone. By reading this, someone out there comes to the realization that you can beat a brain tumor diagnosis. It won't be easy and not everyone beats it, but it can be done. Let me pass on to you all who are fighting. I heard it along the way and and sincerely believe: "It's not what happens to you that matters, but how you react to it." If you get anything from this book, I hope that it is an understanding that attitude makes a huge difference. Try and see the light side of things. Reach ou to your friends and God. Open up your heart and let the people that love you help. Love goes a long way toward healing.

ACKNOWLEDGEMENTS

Wow, this is a tough part. Being a brain tumor survivor is by no means a solo effort, but I consciously chose not to use any names in the telling of my story. There are so many names–family, friends, doctors, technicians, clergy and so on . . . I didn't want anybody to feel more important than anybody else. Obviously my family are on top of that group, but there were people who took me in and carried me. I hope you know who you are and that I have made it well known how much you mean to me. Thank you. If I've sent you a copy of this book, you are probably one of these people.

MY STORY

I got out of college in 1990, as indestructible as any other recent graduate. I got a job–not awful, but not great. I was pretty happy to have a job. It's good to have a job, right? Then all one day I realized I had to get out. I was going to move to San Francisco. I quit my job. After I quit, I had an 'exit interview.' They asked me if I wanted something called "cobra" to extend my health insurance. My initial reaction was–what could happen to me that I would need health insurance. If I got a cold, I'd take SOME MEDICINE. Nothing had ever happened that I'd needed insurance for this far in my life, what was going to change? Then I remembered that someone had told me recently that a broken leg could cost thousands to fix. Now I could see breaking my leg, and I don't think I'd have the cash for that, so I'd might as well get this cobra thing.

MOVING ON

So I told my girlfriend I was leaving, packed up my stuff, and left for San Francisco. I stayed with my college roommate. I got a temp job at a law firm. It was miserable. I had no friends and an awful job, plus my girlfriend and I talked on the phone all the time. She cried. I cried. I had to move back.

MOVING BACK

I packed up my stuff (again) and moved back. My girlfriend said I could stay with her for a while, but it was no guarantee that we were going to stay together. She had told me once that bike couriers were sexy.

BIKE COURIER

I signed up. Now I was a bike courier, not exactly in great physical condition and living in a situation that was not particularly comfortable. I was not an easy person to live with. I was not a very good bike courier, so I didn't make much money. She paid for everything. The bike courier job was becoming more and more difficult. The left side of my body got tired and weak easily. My left leg wasn't doing its part of the job. No wonder I was so slow . . . my right leg was doing all the work. My left hand couldn't use the brake very well. It felt like the courier job was killing me. I was limping around. My speech was slurred. I had become your standard gimp.

DINNER

A friend's parents invited me over for dinner. I never turned down a home cooked meal. They were aghast seeing the gimp I had become. They had known me for many years, and they could see there was definitely something wrong. They told me this.

GIMP

I blew it off, and told them that I had become a bike courier and it was very rough on my body. That is probably true, they agreed, but that didn't account for the fact that the left side of my face was drooping. I went and looked in the mirror. I was horrified. They were right. It looked like the left side of my face was slipping off my skull. As many times that I looked at myself in the mirror every day, I had never noticed. Now I was starting to get nervous. Being a bike courier shouldn't affect my face. But how could something be wrong.

ONLY 25

I was only 25 years old. We had a nice dinner. After dinner, his mother made me promise I would see a doctor right away. Fingers crossed behind my back, I promised. I went back to the house. My girlfriend listened to what they said, and confirmed that yes, I had become a gimp.

BRAINSTORM

We got some friends together and huddled. We brainstormed into the night. It was quite a scene, a group of twenty–something's sitting around throwing out diseases.

WHAT COULD IT BE?

With every new disease, I winced–stroke, fatigue, bells palsy. We talked into the night. But it always came back to-he's only 25, how could he have that. I uncrossed my fingers and decided to see a doctor the next day.

THE TESTS

The doctor also seemed concerned. He gave me all the basic neurological tests that I would experience so many times in the next couple of years.-push your leg against my arm, other side; keep your fingers apart as I squeeze them together; other side. Follow my fingers with your eyes, but don't move your head. Have you have headaches lately?

He told me I had to see a neurologist.

TOMORROW

I told him I would make an appointment sometime in the next couple of weeks.

"No. Make it for tomorrow."

Whoa, tomorrow? What's wrong? He couldn't say for sure. I had to see a neurologist.

I was really lucky and got a great neurologist. He was super nice, which made everything much easier. He also knew what he was talking about. He examined me. Same tests-push this, squeeze that, other side, follow my finger. I needed to get an MRI-magnetic resonance imaging. I needed to get it done, yes, tomorrow.

MAGNETIC RESONANCE IMAGING

So the next day, I reported to the imaging center. It had some sort of ironic name, like happy imaging or something. Their logo was a smiley face. Checking in, they handed me a clipboard with several pages. Fill this out; sign here by the x. don't forget the back sides of the papers. Sign this, initial that, and then bring it back up here. This is another procedure I would become very familiar with. The forms were pretty simple. Name, address, medical background (I had stitches once when I was a kid), medicine allergies (?) asthma (?) Diabetes (?) Claustrophobia (huh?) cancer, what would we be imaging this evening and why (you tell me) do you have any metal in my body? (Am I a robot, is that the question)

THE DUNGEON

I finished the papers (backs also) and brought them to the desk. I had just started reading a doctor's office outdated magazine when a nurse came out and called my name. I followed her down into the dungeon of the imaging center to what appeared to be a dressing room. She told me to take some things off. Shoes, wallet, especially anything metal, watches, coins, belt buckles, necklaces, piercings (piercings ? I'm getting old) and put them in the locker. When this was done, she brought me into the next room. I could see a massive machine that was making loud noises. Apparently there was already somebody in there, because there were two feet sticking out a big hole in the machine. Then I got the talk. Have you ever had a MRI before? No. Are you claustrophobic? (I wonder why they keep asking me this?) Not really. If you were to tie me up in bag, it would freak me out. But not really, no. do you have any metal on or in me? (In me?) Sometimes people have had a job as a metal worker and have a bit of metal in them, or sometimes during surgery, a shunt or some type of other medical device is used. This is a very very strong magnet. If there is a piece of metal in there, it's gonna rip it out (OUCH!).

Well, I've never worked with metal, other than industrial arts class in eighth grade (and I hope I don't have any other bits of metal in me.) I should be good.

She gave me some earplugs (apparently it was a rather loud machine), assured me that they would be right outside the machine if anything went wrong. (I wonder what could go wrong), then explained there was a microphone in the tube, so we would be able to communicate with each other. Also, there would be a tilted mirror above my head, so I would be able to see out the tube (I suppose that was to ease any claustrophobia.)

So they lay me down and pulled a mask over my face, like the one they used for Hannibal Lechter. They explained that I had to make sure not to move my head, even when they pulled me out between scans. That is very important, because if you move your head, it would ruin the shots and I would have to have them redone, if there was a problem at any point, just say something and we'll pull you out.

Then the board I was on started to move into the hole. It was like being on a roller coaster-going up the first big hill, click, click anticipating waiting for what was going to happen next.

Then I was in and the show began. It was tight in there . . . just big enough to stuff an adult in. I can see how people could freak out. If they weren't claustrophobic going in, this might convert them. Then the noise; it was loud in there even with earplugs. The best I can describe the noise is KERPLUNKS and chugga chuggas. The kerplunks were random. Kerplunk . . . . five seconds . . . . kerplunk . . . . two seconds . . . kerplunkkerplunk. The kerplunks were usually followed by a riff of chugga chuggas. I was concentrating on not moving my head. It's harder than it sounds. Every time I took a breath, I was afraid I had ruined the scan. Then I felt like I had to sneeze. I had to hold it in without moving. If couldn't stop the sneeze, then not only would I ruin the scan, but I would smash my face into the Lechter mask right over my face. (If I came out with a bloody face, I would really scare the shit out of the people waiting.)

So the machine kept kerplunking and I kept on taking deep breathes(but not too deep; can't move) so I wouldn't sneeze and so I wouldn't freak out from being in a tube. Then the voice 'Mr. Healy, the next scan is going to be 3 minutes.' (I didn't know that I had been in a particular scan, or how long it had lasted.)

ALIEN ABDUCTION?

It was over. I was sure I had an idea what it was like to be abducted by aliens. Over the next 10 years or so, I would have so many weird tests. This was kinda tame.

Actually, I still couldn't move my head. They had to put me back in the machine. I didn't move my head for about two hours. I even closed my eyes. (I was afraid blinking might be considered moving my head). So then it was over. They pulled me out and said-thank you, we have what we need.-so I asked them what they saw.-we're just technicians, even if we saw something, we couldn't interpret it.-then one guy says-we can't tell, but there is definitely something in there. (Hmmm. I assume he means something other than my brain. I had an appointment with my neurologist tomorrow. I guess I would learn more when I saw him. I called my parents; let them know what I knew, which wasn't much. "Doctors appointment tomorrow. Yes, I'll let you know. I love you too."

Back to the same neurologist. good guy. It's gotta be hard to keep up a happy visage, when most of the time, you're giving people news about the bad things in their head. He was a pediatric neurologist. Most of the doctors that I would see were pediatric; apparently brain tumors are most common in children.

So back to my neurologist, he was really nice, but when he asked me to sit down, I knew there was trouble. He told me that I had a brain tumor.

SURPRISE!

You hear about things like this hitting you like getting punched in the stomach. I didn't faint. I didn't fall out of my chair. I didn't throw up. It was almost like I wasn't that surprised. Someone reminded me later than in high school I used to tell people that I would probably get killed by a brain tumor one day because I had read that illnesses tended to strike your strongest asset.

It wasn't huge, but it was on the brain stem, which is a bad place to be because it made it very difficult to operate on. Still, he wanted me to see a brain surgeon at the local university that my HMO had contracted for neurosurgery. Then he told me that if I was alive in ten years, technology would be advanced enough, that it could probably be removed easily. And he thought that I would be. (Sure enough.) Appointment with the surgeon, always tomorrow.

THE JUNGLE

When I got to the office, I checked in and got the requisite paperwork (insurance, background) then had my typical doctor's office typical wait (I wound up getting a lot of reading done-I learned to always bring a book to doctors offices, because reading five year old popular mechanics just wasn't doing it for me . . . .)When it was my turn, I was escorted down the dark halls to the office where he waited in his leather chair (it was like apocalypse now-through the jungle to eventually meet up with him. We said hello then put my MRIs into the light machines on his wall (THWACK< THWACK< THWACK<, another sound I would become very familiar with)

He explained the difficulty of the 'situation' because of the location of the lesion (I still don't know why I they call it a lesion) I might want to consider alternative options, but these options (chemotherapy and radiation) wouldn't be as effective as surgery. He told me that he had done many surgeries like this successfully. He ran down his qualifications and background, and offered me a list of his past patients as references.

SECOND OPINION

Something I learned along the way is that you always should get a second opinion. I didn't want to offend my surgeon so I was hesitant. I was told over and over that it is standard practice and you won't offend anyone. Furthermore, it is vital in finding the best treatment for you. So I proceeded on a country-wide tour of brain experts. I saw doctors at John Hopkins, UCSF, and a few others and the opinion was always the same . . . "boy, you need some surgery." So, back to Georgetown.

FIRST SURGERY

I reported to the first surgery of my life early one morning for my preparation. I had shaved my own head the night before (it wasn't pretty, but I figured they would take care of anything I missed. When I got there, they greeted me and walked me through a corridor of moaning people waiting to be cut up. It was kind of shocking. I felt like I was walking through a haunted cemetery or a theme park for the raiders of the lost ark. They brought me to a room, sat me down, and my pre-op 'interview' began. Have you ever had surgery before (no.) do you know what your surgeon is going to be doing today? (Vaguely, yes. I know there is going to be a saw and then a knife and then some minute cutting and removing and then, hopefully, in a few hours my family and friends will be standing around me smiling and commenting how much I look like Frankenstein . . .) um that is more or less the plan. (Some people handle humor better than others, but I figure I'm the one going under the saw, I can be in whatever mood I want.) There are a few things that I want you to try and remember. When you wake up from surgery you're going to be very confused (no shit) there is going to be a tube in your throat that is going to be uncomfortable (hurt). Do not touch the tube! It is important not to touch it. If you try to touch it you will be restrained. (Ok, I'll try to remember) there will be people all around you. They are gonna talk to you. Probably ask you some questions. What is your name? How many fingers am I holding up? If you get these questions wrong, you are fucked. (Ok, she didn't say that.)

Then they took me to a bed, and put some devices on my legs that keep the blood moving, to avoid blood clots. they put the needle in me and tell me I'll be asleep soon, and could I please sign this paperwork so they can go forward with the surgery.(aw c'mon, I've got a needle in my arm and a tumor in my head hmm, wonder what I'm gonna do now?) I take a quick look at it.(blah blah blah you can't sue the hospital for this and that. Understand the risk blah blah) ok, I'll sign it. Scribble scribble. And then she leaves.

NEXT THING I KNOW

I am being rolled on my gurney toward my room. Wouldn't you know, the first thing I did was grab at that fucking tube in my throat. I know they warned me, but it hurt like hell and I just wanted to adjust it a little. (They didn't say I couldn't adjust it.) when I reached for it, the nurses quickly grabbed my arms and tied them down with some white fluffy restraints. (It wasn't at all as sexy as it sounds.) Before I had entered the hospital, I had developed the annoying habit of answering a question with the same question. So when they pulled me out on the gurney, and after they had tied my hands down, the nurse asked,

"How do you feel?"

I answered," How do you feel?" so then everybody knew that I was okay. Then the doctor asked me if I knew my name (john), who is the president? (Clinton-damn, should have had some fun and said 'Jefferson,' which wouldn't have been completely inaccurate.) What day of the week was it (that was a hard one, but I asked someone before I went in, and I remembered so . . . Friday. Then the basic tests. Squeeze my fingers, push against my arm with your leg, and Follow my finger. I passed them all. The doctor was happy, and told my parents that everything turned out all right despite some difficulties during surgery. Alright, my ass, was my brain's response. That night I had the worst headaches I've ever had. The only way I can describe the pain is to say that my head had been filled with throbbing concrete. I had to keep my head completely still and hold my forehead against the metal restraint on the side of my bed.

LOOK AT ME

It still amazes me that they can cut the skin across your forehead, pull your face skin down, saw a hole in your skull, slide in through all the folds of meat and remove a substance that has to look like gravy on a mud pie THEN staple and sew everything back to look like a human again. I wasn't ever a particularly pretty fellow, so I am just amazed to look in a mirror and see something that resembles a human . . . .

PAIN KILLERS

You'd think that I would get some really powerful pain killers after brain surgery. I had heard about a painkiller pump that allowed you to self-administer pain killers. But instead, they brought me Tylenol with codeine.

You've gotta be kidding. Look at me. I can barely blink my eyes without lightning shooting through my head. Maybe you don't understand what my brain just went through . . . . no luck. In fact, I would only be able to get the Tylenol every 3 hours. So I spent the night begging for more Tylenol. "Sorry, Mr. Healy, doctors orders."

So, when the doctor showed up on his rounds the next morning believe me, he got a piece of my mind.(again) I told him that after last night, I was going to need a pump so that I could self-administer some decent pain-killer. Yes, I probably would pull a muscle in my thumb, but otherwise, I don't see why it would be a problem. Sorry, the problem during surgery probably caused more post operative pain then he anticipated (you think?) then it was explained to me that powerful narcotic painkillers would mask any symptoms that they would need to pick up on that would indicate problems. He would increase the strength of my Tylenol. Ahh Tylenol again-I just had brain surgery, not the flu!

FEAR

Sure, there is the idea of death, but I think I had come to terms with that. I am scared about living as a vegetable. Also, I am worried about being awake under the anesthesia. So you feel everything, but you can't let anyone know. You try to scream; you try to blink. Nothing. There is a better chance that a meteor is gonna hit you in your Achilles heal, but fears are fears.

LIVING WILL

I make sure to have a living will written before the surgery. Don't want to be kept alive by machines. Everyone should have one of these prepared, just in case. You're thinking you're too young to need one of those. Believe me, I was only 25, when I was diagnosed, and I luckily had the time to think about these things . . . . As long as there are buses and crosswalks, you never know . . .

So, after I've been lounging in my room for a few days, the surgeon comes in with my parents (that can't be good.) they tell me that everything went pretty well, although there was a small brain injury that could cause some pain in recovering. He wasn't able to remove it all, but he got a good chunk of it. But it's so slow growing that I shouldn't run across any problems. He'd like to see me have a course of radiation here at the university. Otherwise, everything went well.

A couple of weeks later, I get a call from the surgeon's office asking me if I could come in for a quick appointment (that can't be good) So, of course, I can be there . . . how's tomorrow? So he got a good chunk, but apparently not enough for an accurate biopsy. So he needed to get that to confirm the stage of the tumor. He was almost positive it was a low-grade Astrocytoma, but he wanted to make sure. So he needed more. I had a couple of options. He could do a stereo-tactic procedure (big needle through the skull to the tumor), or a regular surgery. The advantage to the regular surgery being that if there was a problem (problem? Punctured blood vessel), it could be dealt with immediately. If a similar problem happened during a stereotactic procedure, my skull would have to be opened without any planning (ah, planning is good). So I thought about it called my parents, thought some more, then despite my fear of a vegetable outcome, or the not all the way under phenomenon, I would take the 'another surgery option. Time to make sure the clippers still worked . . .

SUPPORT

But before the next surgery, someone told me about a brain tumor support group. I didn't really think it would be helpful, but someone had gone to the trouble of finding out info and telling me about it. Plus, people were starting to be concerned about my 'mental state' (hmm, ya think), so maybe if I went to this, they would get off my back.

So I reported to the generic conference room at a local hospital. There was a decent sized group, maybe 20 people. I took a seat at the big conference sized table. I didn't have to say . . . . 'Hi. My name is john. I have a brain tumor.' We all introduced ourselves. The group members varied in states of deterioration. There were a few wheelchairs, a few droolers, lots of slurred speech. There was one distinct feature of the group. I was the youngest. So, my first reaction was that I didn't fit in . . . Then everybody started telling their stories. Most of the people had gone through multiple surgeries, chemo and/or radiation and all sorts of rehab and treatment. Then the group started asking questions about different therapies (I had heard about most of them), and people's stories about their experiences . . . (Different doctors, different medicines, different programs) so my second lesson was good. You can go through a lot of shit, and still be alive, and these people were fighters. I guess I did learn something-you can't just lie down and let it win, you have to fight. I also learned something else. Something that I realize more and more everyday. Someone said that you have to accept that your body will never be the same. I think he might have been talking to me. I was obviously in denial to some degree. He wanted me to know that I wasn't always going to be able to do the things I've taken for granted(I discover something everyday that I can't do any more: catch a ball, cut my food, swim) so, I had learned a few things, but I wasn't going back. I felt out of place because of the age difference. I thought brain tumors were most common in children (I guess it would be odd to send a five year old to the group, but really all I wanted was a few women my age–maybe that wasn't the best gene pool for me to be fishing.)

SURGERY#2

So I went through the routine again. A routine I'd rather not become familiar with. (too late). Shave my head, show up nice and early, or early at least, make sure the surgeon wasn't drinking the night before, get poked with the appropriate needles, say good bye to my family and friends (hopefully not forever . . .), sign some papers even though I have no idea what they say, say some prayers, then bye . . .

I wake up. They give me the squeeze this push that-apparently I am not crippled.(take me to my room. I'm tired) there are lots of faces around me-a few tears. The doctor comes in to make sure I am doing ok. He tells me that he got a big enough chunk for an accurate biopsy(I hope so.) I ask everyone to leave so I can relax. Really I just want to see if I get HBO on this TV (I must be all right)

RADIATION

So my follow up check up shows that everything had gone fine for the most part. A follow up mri shows that there is still a big wad still in there. Doc says I should get some radiation. Sounds good. I ask my neuro what he thinks. He concurs. So an appointment is set up for, yes, tomorrow. Once again I go to the university. They explain the process to me. Apparently I would come in every day for a month and have radiation shot into my head. The goal of the radiation was not short term. Radiation was to keep the cells from dividing, which would hopefully stop any future growth. I was going to have to be patient. (Can do) the doctor I met with didn't have much to do with the every day procedures. He was just kept up to date on what was going on. Day to day would be handled by some technicians.

Technicians can make all the difference. You're not in a particularly good mood when you go in, so it helps if someone has a little happy to share. So thank you to all you friendly techs who helped me on my way. My radiation techs were particularly friendly. They told me that they would do some setting(aiming) and would mark the spots with tiny tattoo pricks(I asked if I could get a naked woman, and you could just aim at her . . . . bellybutton. no can do. Just your standard dot. Pinprick size–boring!)so they put me on the table, and spent some time pushing my head an inch this way or that while looking into a computer and following a red beam of light. It took a while (take your time-don't want any errant beams bouncing around the room) when I was in the exact right spot, they pin–prick the tattoo, now I am marked. (Like a creature on animal planet) they sit me down and explain the process. I come in and lay down, they adjust me so the red beam lines are pointed at the dots, and then zap zap. All done. I'm gonna lose hair where the beam goes in. I may feel nauseous. I will probably experience fatigue now and for years in the future. We can validate your parking stub. Any questions? (no,) No? then we'll see you tomorrow.(Thank you. I'd mention your names, but I learned later that the two of you were having an affair. Plus I haven't written any other names.)

So I went in for my treatments. Zap zap. Went in every day. Pretty easy. One day I rode my bike just so I could hold it over future children (you think you have it tough, when I was your age I had to ride my bike to radiation treatments . . .) so it went. I was tired but I always had been.) The hair fell off my right temple, giving me a radiation mullet, I got a little nauseous (I wasn't throwing up in public or anything, so it wasn't much)

When it was over, I went and had yet another MRI. I still had a brain tumor.

Hoping the radiation had taken care of any more growth, I was a new man. Healthy and happy and ready to take on the world. I got another job . . . still a so so job, but I was happy to be back in rotation. I was having MRIs about every 6 months. About 3 or 4 years later. Somebody pointed out that I was limping a bit. People limp, right? No problem. People no problem. Me-problem.

HOLISTIC

By all means, read, research and do some things that sound like they could help. Remember that saying–god helps those that help themselves. I tried a few different things . . . . visualization, meditation and I even went vegan for a while. I developed a little mantra to inspire my white blood cells(KILL KILL KILL CHOMP CHOMP CHOMP STARVE STARVE STARVE STOMP STOMP STOMP i would sit in the dark and repeat my little battle cry as I visualized my white blood cells destroying the unwanted invader–by any means necessary)

BRIAN TUMOR

One of the funniest things that has happened came at a regular doctors check up between surgeries. I was waiting in the chairs to be called in. there are a bunch of people waiting. The nurse comes out with her clipboard, looks down and yells out 'BRIAN TUMOR.' Everyone in the waiting room looks around. I was thinking-what an unfortunate name.-then she stops, smiles, and says, 'sorry, that's John Healy with a brain tumor.' Oops. She was very embarrassed and very apologetic.

So I'm having some pretty bad (the most awful I've ever experienced) headaches (that can't be good) I refuse to believe that it could be happening again, but I call the neuro anyway. Another MRI. chugga chugga. Thwack thwack. Looks like you have to visit the surgeon again. (Shit) the problem is that 'my' surgeon was gone. He accepted a position at a hospital in Rhode Island. Head of Pediatric Neurosurgery. Not too shabby. So next brain surgeon in line for me. Once again, luck of the draw. I pulled a really nice guy. Just hoping his surgical skills are as good as his personality. My case is a little better known now, so when I get to his office, I am like a regular.

Apparently, my 'case' had already been explained to my new surgeon by the director of the department who had remembered me. The new doc explained that there was some new technology that was gonna assist in this surgery-an inter-operative CAT scan that would help guide the 'knife' to cut out the bad stuff and stay away from the fragile stuff. (Sounds good to me). ok lets schedule a surgery. Not tomorrow (finally), but maybe two weeks. (Ink me in doc. Lets do this thing)

So the night before arrives, and I'm ready to shave my head and say my prayers when the phone rings. It's the hospital. Inter-operative scan machine is broken . . . (Shit . . . Let's not do this thing) just my luck . . . they need to reschedule. Maybe a few days, maybe a week. (Whatever it takes . . . I'm not going anywhere) I'll just shave my head again, and prepare myself mentally . . . . again. So déjà vu. Night before, phone rings (you gotta be kidding me . . .) yup, not working . . . need another week. Err to the safe side, I guess, but my brain is gonna explode before they can get to it.

So another week, night before . . . no phone calls, just prayers and a touch up on the shave job.

I go in the next morning and do the same routine . . . pre-op talk, surgery robe, circulation boots, sign the papers, ask someone what day of the week it is . . . by bye see ya later(once again, hopefully)

On the gurney. Tears and smiles . . . familiar faces . . . must not be dead. But this time I get a new test.

Count backwards from 100 by 7s. oh man, you gotta be kidding don't think I could do that easily beforehand. I don't know if my violated brain can handle this one, oh, I get it, this is a joke. Yes, I still have a sense of humor. Didn't cut that out . . . for real . . . 100 . . . 93 . . . . 86 . . . . Clinton . . . Friday . . . john . . . sorry . . . where was I . . . . 79 . . . . 72 . . . blah blah . . . Get them all . . . yup alive is the verdict. Sure hope this is it. Did you get what you need? Good. No more. Please. Uh, wait. I can't really move that well for the tests. Pull this, push that. Not so good. Faces are more concerned than teary. What happened? Later, it was explained to me (through a haze) that there was a significant brain injury. I'm beginning to think there is always some sort of brain injury. I imagine it's pretty delicate in there; if someone coughs in the parking lot, through some universal motion, it touches the blade-one of many possible paths. At this point I cannot shit, sit, walk, or talk . . . . but I'm still around. I can work with that.

So then it gets tricky. My insurance (HMO) decides future hospital care would not help to improve my situation, so I should be sent to a 'home' where I can be taken care of. (No way!) My family and friends recognize this diagnosis, and decide its not over yet (god, I love them) so after phone calls, arguments, lawyers, and money, a decision is made that I will be sent to a local rehab hospital. Fortunately, one of the best in the country happened to be in my backyard.

REHAB

I get transferred to my new home via ambulance (I was hoping to be escorted by a couple of black SUVs, but not from a HMO–don't think so . . .) I had been told a lot of good things about this rehab hospital, and since talking, walking, eating (basically functioning) weren't my strengths of mine at the moment, I was curious to see what they could do with me. I don't think I realize what kind of shape I was in at this point. I only remember being a sarcastic wise ass, and there are certainly moments where that side is illuminated, but I thinking drooling moaning pointing me was how I was admitted. I saw a note I had tried to write my first week or so in rehab. It was completely incomprehensible scrawling. It looked like I had tried to draw it with my foot. So drooling and moaning they took me. Let's see what they could do . . .

They took me to my new 'space.' No cushy remote controlled color TV here. I was in a new world. My space was a bed surrounded by sheets in an auditorium full of hanging sheets. Asylum is the word that came to mind as I looked around . . . . and listened. There was more moaning than a whorehouse. Right next to my area was a guy who moaned over and over maaaryyyy7 marrryyyseven. Wow. I thought I was in bad shape. He had been in a motorcycle accident (no helmet)

So then my retraining began. Sitting, walking slowly, and using my fingers. I have always been blessed by friends-so I spent a good amount of my time interacting with visitors.

CARAVAN

By this time, a 'group,' almost like a gypsy caravan, had established itself and followed me from facility to facility. My visitors were a good group of people-a mix of friends, relatives, Parent's friends, people from my past, priests, girlfriend's parents, coworkers.

FONDLE

It's really nice having so many loving people around. You'd be amazed how much fondling you can get away with when you're in a hospital bed. Nobody smacks a guy with surgical staples in his head. A friend asked me—why do you want to grab my breast. I said, its not that I want to, I need to.

FUNERAL

Having a big group of visitors gives you the unique perspective of being a guest at your own funeral. You see the look on people's faces when they first see you lying there, sickly and hooked up to a dozen machines. It's as if they've just given the eulogy.

So the 'waiting room' crew was always right on the sideline waiting to step up and offer their special encouragement, and everybody brought presents. I love presents, but when you're laid up, it's just harder to appreciate them.

BARNEY

One of my presents was a helium Barney head. The helium kept it on the ceiling for a couple of hours, but by the middle of the night the helium started to fade and it was hanging real low, plus the ventilation in my space pushed it so it was hanging right in front of my face. It's a very scary thing to wake to a face full of Barney. Good thing it was the Neuro ward and not the cardiac ward, because there would have been a heart attack. When I woke up from a nap to find Barney hanging out inches from my face, I swatted him hard and had him removed from my area.

TICKLE

Part of my daily routine was urination. For most of my time in the hospital, they had me piss in a plastic container so they could test and measure my 'output.' When we got to the rehab hospital, they eventually let me hit the pisser-with an escort of course. My escort was a male nurse. The poor man's job was to lug my big ass to the urinal and hold me there 'til the job was done. He was about half my size, a third my weight, and I was having stage fright, so the poor man had to stand there and hold me up at the urinal.

Then one day during this 'workout,' he showed me he had learned something new. I can just see him calling some old professor of his . . . . 'I don't know what to do. It takes this big guy so long to piss, sometimes I don't know if I can hold him.'

He pulled out a piece of toilet paper while he was holding me up and tickled the head of my penis. it made me piss. It was awesome. He could take me back to my space without fear of dropping me in the toilet.

I was one of my biggest dangers in the hospital. I was in no condition, physically or mentally, to be going exploring, but I insisted on taking off. i don't know where I went or what I did, but I would always set off a small panic. He escaped again! They would find me sitting in my wheelchair alone in some corridor. No one knew I could make it that far on my own.

LOCKDOWN

Security obviously had to be stepped up. So the inevitable happened, one day my family showed up after their breakfast to find me in a cage. I immediately started rattling the cage, screeching and tossing my feces. Ok, it wasn't like that. I danced and they put singles in my diaper. Ok, it wasn't so much a cage as it was a baby's crib, but it was confinement. Seeing me in a cage freaked a lot of my people out. Now that I was in lock down, there were no more joy rides for me. I had to find my fun inside the cage. My substantial meal of the day consisted of having a can of ensure poured into a tube that went directly my stomach. I craved solid food desperately-and let them know whenever possible. For some reason, I particularly craved waffles. 'my kingdom for a waffle,' I remember saying at least once. But, of course, you couldn't get a waffle down the tube. So, from the privacy of my cage, I yanked it out. I'm not sure how it was anchored, but it had to be tied down somehow. It still makes me cringe to think of my self pulling out the tube, ignoring pain and consequences to allay my stubborn disposition. But out it came, and a small circular scar, about the size of a dime, remained to remind me.

I seemed to have strange little uncommon problems along the way. Towards the end of my stay, I had to wear a reddish/pinkish plastic gown to warn nurses that I had some sort of contagious condition. I was already paranoid, and now I had to wear a pink plastic robe. I might have well been wearing a boa made of rubber gloves, and then they decided they would bring me and my people for waffles. (IHOP) pink robe and special needs bus, we were off.

IHOP

We showed up in their parking lot like a school bus of thirsty elementary school students at a 7-11. The poor families having breakfast must have been horrified as we rolled, limped and staggered off our bus towards them, like zombies from our graves. I was super excited and led the way in my cautionary red robe. The meal went over well. I almost cried over my blueberry syrup. I must be getting better to enjoy such things. Look at what therapy has prepared me for.

Therapy was going well, therefore it was getting easier. Classes and learning were spread out and the subjects of what I was learning were simpler and they were easier for me to do. So rather than doing something like speaking out loud, I would practice getting in and out of a car (a technique I use to this day-some things you never forget)

NURSES AND THERAPISTS

First of all, god bless them. Who wants to do what they do? They have to be so patient and knowledgeable. God bless 'em. But don't let them fool you. There is some sadism in there too. They know they have a room full of sleep deprived, on-the-edge, full of pain relief medicine people under there complete control. They have some fun too. I'm sure every once in a while one will say to another something like "I'm going to over in that corner and dance around in this rainbow afro wig. If anybody says anything, deny it. "no mr. Johnson, there isn't anyone over here. I can see this area from the desk. We all thought we were crazy. I know I did.

NIGHTMARE

I had a recurring nightmare where they rounded us all up in the middle of the night and put us in a big box where we were all chopped up. When we were just mush we were put in big plastic trash bags and sold to fast food joints. This very real seeming dream went on until my best friend showed up one night, threw me over his shoulder, kicked down the door and saved me.

FALL IN LOVE

I did something that I recommend to anyone that finds themselves hospitalized. I fell in love with one of my nurses. I didn't harass, grope, or generally get nasty around her. I just adored her. She had the raspiest sexiest voice I had ever heard. Even if I couldn't see so well, I could still find comfort in her voice. She was good to me. I constantly fed her adoration. My family got to know her and liked her also, and was able to communicate with her because they could tell I trusted her. After I had been out of the hospital a year or so, I went back to visit her; I didn't recognize her at all.

VISION

There are 12 nerves that run down the brain stem. They are called the cranial nerves. They control different functions in the body. The third of these nerves is the ocular motor nerve. Just like it sounds, it controls eye movement. My third nerve got a little beat up causing a condition called third nerve palsy. This caused my right eye to point out to the right a bit, which caused my poor brain some confusion. This confusion came in the form of double vision. I kept my head bent over, my left ear almost on my left shoulder. This made the two images look a little closer together, but made me look like a freak. Eventually, someone figured out I was having this vision problem and gave me an eye patch(ay, matey . . . . sounds a lot cooler than it is . . . imagine strapping a black Frisbee to your face with some black elastic string . . .) this vision problem made my time at rehab even more confusing. Now, along with the sleep deprivation, the pain, and the medication, I had screwy vision. Now the hallucinations got even worse. I was in a sail boat, a spider web. There were cats running across the floors. No, they were rats. Was that my friend ray that just walked in?

MEMORY

I almost feel like I remember enjoying being in rehab. I was flirting with my nurses, groping my visitors, relearning life skills, keeping a social life with the waiting room. But really the things I've related to you were told to me. So my story is 'passed down' to you-almost like a folk tale of days passed.

TAKE AWAY

What I want you to "get" from my little tale here is: a brain tumor diagnosis is not a death sentence. Try to keep a positive attitude. It's really hard, but so many people just drop dead from an aneurism or a heart attack. You have been given a chance to fight. Lean on your family and friends. Reach out to God. Don't give up. Fight. Laugh. Joke around. It's not gonna be easy, but don't give up . . .

NOW WHAT

So I managed to survive a couple of surgeries. Now what?? I've got a bunch of scars and dents in my skull, not to mention an eye patch (AY MATEY) Am I really supposed to get out there and try to get laid, work and function with people? The guidance upon leaving rehab was don't hit your head. REALLY? Because I was planning on finding the first brick wall available and challenging it to a head butting contest . . . So I assume karma has some sort of rule that I will never get sick again and I will have nothing but good luck. Note to self: buy a lottery ticket. Hello world! Here comes tumor boy! Kinda sounds like a lead in to another book right? Mmm. Maybe.

BULLY PULPIT

This is my book, my platform so I'd like to give a big ole "shout out" to my little sister. If you're ever wondering if a sibling loves you, get sick. My sister came through like a champion. She is the reason I am not rotting in a home right now. Thanks Jo Jo.

CPSIA information can be obtained at www.ICGtesting.com
Printed in the USA
BVOW071615041012

302175BV00002B/45/P

9 781479 712205